THE HEYDAY OF THE **WARSHIPS**

Hugh Dady

Ian Allan
PUBLISHING

Front cover: No D834 *Pathfinder* approaches the 'Avenue' at Bradford-on-Avon with train 7V02, the 08.00 Poole–Severn Tunnel Junction, on 21 September 1966. The train was routed via Southampton, Salisbury and Westbury. *The Rev Alan Newman* (Kodachrome II, 25ASA)

Back cover: No D603 *Conquest* leaves Newton Abbot with the up 'Mayflower' (8.30am Plymouth–Paddington) on 15 July 1959. *R. C. Riley* (Kodachrome, 8ASA)

Previous page: Newquay on Saturday 17 June 1967. Centre stage is No D800 *Sir Brian Robertson* about to leave with the 08.55 to Newcastle. No D861 *Vigilant* stands adjacent with the 11.45 to York while No D6308 awaits developments as the station pilot. *David Pool* (Kodachrome II, 25ASA)

Below: Inspiration for the 'Warships' were the very successful 'V200s' of Deutsche Bundesbahn. Last of the prototype series of 'V200s', No 220.005-3, enters Neckargemund on 10 March 1970 with train E1646, the 09.28 Wurzburg–Pirmasens. *Peter Gray* (Kodachrome II, 25ASA)

First published 2008

ISBN (10) 0 7110 3242 4
ISBN (13) 978 0 7110 3242 2

© Ian Allan Publishing 2008

Published by Ian Allan Publishing
an imprint of Ian Allan Publishing Ltd, Hersham, Surrey, KT12 4RG

Printed in England by Ian Allan Publishing Ltd, Hersham, Surrey, KT12 4RG

Code: 0803/B

Visit the Ian Allan Publishing website at www.ianallanpublishing.com

Introduction

As a weak, watery sun climbed above the Bristol skyline on Sunday 3 December 1972, it seems unlikely that anyone gave thought to the events unfolding on the Western Region of British Rail. With the cloud base gathering in the late morning of that winter Sunday, No 821 *Greyhound* returned to Bristol Bath Road after completion of a Sunday engineering possession near Stoke Gifford. The locomotive was then assigned to train 6Z10, an additional working of the normal weekday 4B10 service to Plymouth, laid on to carry the extra Christmas mail and parcels traffic.

No 821 left the depot shortly after 15.00 and backed onto the train leaving behind a handful of already stored or withdrawn sisters. *Greyhound*'s journey west was slow even by the standards of parcels trains at the time, with numerous lengthy station stops to sort the pre-Christmas traffic. It was after 22.00 when the locomotive drew into Plymouth North Road with the last 'Warship'-hauled train on British Rail and nearly midnight by the time it arrived home at Laira, the final depot to which the 'Warships' were allocated. The class had quietly slipped away and such was the level of interest at the time that it took several days for the few enthusiasts to realise what had happened.

Looking back, it is hard to believe that a class that had spearheaded the Modernisation Plan on the WR would end their BR career without even a single farewell special — few significant locomotive classes have joined this rather exclusive club. It is true that the locomotives had occasionally been requested on a tiny handful of trips but none could be described as a farewell run. On 16 April 1972 the organisers of the joint Plymouth Railway Circle / Great Western Society trip to the Bluebell Railway requested 'Warship' haulage, to which BR readily agreed. Eight months before the last was switched off, it was the closest the class would ever come to any formal farewell. Front line work continued through the summer but by the autumn of 1972 the handful of survivors were usually relegated to freight services including the heavy stone trains from the Mendip quarries to Gatwick and Merstham in connection with motorway construction.

Because of the strong family connection with the original five A1A 'Warships', I have included a handful of the North British Class 22s or 'D63xxs', as they were known at the time; it is only in recent years that the term 'Baby Warship' has come to be used, this being an obvious description, because the design effectively represented a 'D6xx' cut in half.

In just 14 years the 'Warships' had come and gone, dressed in a host of livery variations in each of the main green, maroon and blue phases. Fortunately a handful of photographers continued to record in colour the ever-changing railway scene, which today provides much interest for modellers and preservationists alike. My thanks go to all those who have allowed me to search through their collections of both slides and working documents during a project that has brought back many fond memories of a class which was very much a personal favourite.

Hugh Dady
Dawlish
January 2008

Below: No D604 *Cossack* leads a North British B-B 'Warship' across Chacewater Viaduct on 8 June 1963 with the up TPO from Penzance to Paddington.
Michael Messenger (Perutz CT18 50ASA)

3

First of the A1A-A1A North British 'Warships', No D600 *Active*, passes Swindon with a test train on 28 February 1958, ushering in a new era on the Western Region. No D600 had been ordered by the British Transport Commission (BTC) in 1955 but represented something of a compromise. The WR had sent a high-level delegation to see the compact and powerful 'V200s' built by Krauss-Maffei operating on German Federal Railways and was in no doubt about what it wanted. The BTC, which had overall responsibility for the British Railways Modernisation Plan, favoured a more conventional approach and was subject to political pressure to support British manufacturers. The North British Locomotive Co already had a licence agreement with MAN Diesels of Augsburg and Voith at Heidenheim and was thus given a contract for a pilot series of locomotives. The design and method of construction was influenced by Nos 10000 and 10001, designed by the LMS, and, whilst this resulted in a handsome locomotive, its bulk was a far cry from the lightweight design of the 'V200s'. *Trevor Owen* (Kodachrome, 8ASA)

Active was joined in March 1958 by sister locomotive No D601, named after the aircraft-carrier *Ark Royal*. The two locomotives remained under the care of the commissioning team at Swindon until June, both locomotives making journeys down into Cornwall as part of the extensive testing programme. On week commencing 16 June No D601 took up a duty that involved the down working of the prestigious 'Cornish Riviera Express', which the locomotive worked each day from Paddington as far as Plymouth. This is the view on the Thursday of that week as *Ark Royal* emerges from Dainton Tunnel with the 10.30am Paddington–Penzance. Today's photographers may like to note that, while the dull June weather has not changed over the years, the film speed for colour work was just 8ASA, so that even with the fastest lens of the day a shutter speed of no more than 1/60 would have been possible — hence the need for panning. *Trevor Owen* (Kodachrome, 8ASA)

Left: No D601 *Ark Royal* approaches Hanwell & Elthorne with the down 'Cornish Riviera Limited' on 6 October 1958. Of interest is the wording on the headboard compared with the picture on page 5. The term 'Limited' had been used since 1906 to denote the then longest non-stop run between Paddington and Plymouth, but in the early 'Fifties the name was shortened to 'Cornish Riviera'. 'Limited' made a return in 1956 but was replaced in April 1958 by the new title 'Cornish Riviera Express' ready for the diesels to take over. Within the railway, the train continued to be known as the 'Limited' despite additional stops. Perhaps the crew had gone to the back of the stores at Old Oak that day, for photographs of a diesel carrying the 'Limited' headboard are rare. *Ken Wightman* (Kodachrome, 8ASA)

Right: No D603 *Conquest* crosses Hungerford Common with train 054, the 8.15am Perranporth–Paddington, on 4 July 1959. Although the early 'Warships' have often received a poor press in enthusiast publications, the drivers who worked with them appreciated their smooth ride, with none of the problems in bogie design that troubled both the later, Swindon-designed 'Warships' and the larger 'Westerns'. They were built like tanks, as British Railways found out as early as December 1959, when No D602 *Bulldog* was involved in a collision with No 5028 *Llantilio Castle* at Devonport Junction; the 'Castle' was damaged beyond economic repair, while No D602 suffered little more than a bent buffer and superficial damage to the front valance. *R. C. Riley* (Kodachrome, 8ASA)

Although published before, this historic view of No D800 *Sir Brian Robertson* returning from its inaugural public run is simply too noteworthy to omit. At last the WR had got what it really wanted — a lightweight, scaled-down version of the 'V200' with Maybach engines to fit the UK loading-gauge. In deference to the Chairman of the BTC the WR Board rejected the originally allocated name of *Vanguard* and invited Sir Brian Robertson to name the locomotive at Paddington on 14 July 1958. The following day it worked the down 'Cornish Riviera Express' with invited guests as far as Plymouth, where the VIP party were scheduled to watch a locomotive change for the onward journey to Penzance before visiting Laira shed.

No D800 performed very well, achieving a 10min-early arrival at Plymouth. There, according to Dick Riley's notes, attention had to be quickly diverted, as the replacement No D601 had managed to get no further from Laira shed than Lipson Junction, and a grimy 'Hall' had hurriedly to be substituted. Dick was in position at Cowley Bridge Junction on the following afternoon for No D800's return with the 1.20pm Penzance–Paddington on 16 July 1958. A fitter in smart white boiler suit may just be seen leaning from the second engine-room window. *R.C. Riley* (Kodachrome, 8ASA)

Before Pilot Scheme Nos D800-2 had turned a wheel an order was placed for a production run at Swindon with engines uprated from 2,000 to 2,200hp and an alphabetical sequence of names honouring Royal Naval warships. This is the second of the production batch, No D804 *Avenger*, passing Burlescombe under clear signals and about to cross the Devon/Somerset border with the 7.30am Penzance–Manchester on 17 June 1959. Visually, the only obvious difference when compared with the Pilot Scheme locomotives lies in the double-length handrails under the front cab windows. Steam-age brackets remain for carrying the stencilled three-digit train reporting number, while the two white discs correctly denote an express passenger train. *K. L. Cook / Rail Archive Stephenson* (Kodachrome, 8ASA)

Left: A fascinating view inside 'A' Shop at Swindon, recorded on 3 May 1959. No D806 is in 'shop' green, nearly complete and awaiting a first coat of BR locomotive green. No D600 stands alongside, receiving its first major stripdown after a year in service. Part of the alloy nose has been removed, and the two fuel tanks (of differing capacities) can be seen in front of the locomotive. The 'D6xxs' carried the fuel tanks within the locomotive body, while the later 'D8xx' series followed the design of the 'V200s', with the fuel tanks slung below the body amidships. *Trevor Owen* (Kodachrome, 8ASA)

Above: Just one month old, No D805 *Benbow* pauses at Taunton on 16 June 1959 with the down 'Royal Duchy' (1.30pm Paddington–Penzance). Everything is as it should be, with the gleaming locomotive carrying the cream-backed headboard that included the arms of the Duchy of Cornwall and destination boards on each of the smart rake of chocolate-and-cream Mk 1 coaches. As with all new B-B 'Warships' the buffer-beam and coupling apron is finished in a slightly orange-red colour that matched the shade used for the nameplate backing. By 1963 the specification had clearly changed, and locomotives outshopped after attention at Swindon were given pillarbox-red buffer-beams, this colour being extended to nameplates upon repainting. *K. L. Cook / Rail Archive Stephenson* (Kodachrome, 8ASA)

Left: Running at speed just to the west of Twyford on the approach to Sonning Cutting is No D801 *Vanguard* at the head of train 332, the down 'Torbay Express', on Saturday 5 December 1959. No D801 had been chosen to undertake controlled road tests in October 1958 between Didcot and Bristol to establish the characteristics of the class under various conditions. The Institute of Locomotive Engineers paper presented on 17 November 1959 recorded that the maximum speed for which test data was obtained was 103mph. In the early months of operation some drivers were keen to exploit this, but the honeymoon was brought to an abrupt close within a year. Concerns over the lateral movement of the bogie, giving some lively riding, resulted in the Civil Engineer's imposing an 80mph ceiling until the problem was resolved. *Trevor Owen (Kodachrome, 8ASA)*

Above: Slogging up Hemerdon Bank without assistance is No D808 *Centaur* with the up 'Cornish Riviera Express' (9.45am Penzance–Paddington) on Good Friday (31 March) 1961. *John Beckett (Kodachrome, 8ASA)*

13

Above: No D603 *Conquest* has just crossed Penadlake Viaduct on the climb through the Glynn Valley east of Bodmin Road with the up 'Cornish Riviera Express', the 10am Penzance-Paddington, on 5 June 1961. Starting with No D602, additional horizontal handrails were fitted to the front of the class, visible to the left and right of the headboard in this view. While Nos D600 and D601 had engines and transmissions manufactured in Germany, the later three had a significantly higher proportion of British-manufactured equipment made under licence agreements. The UK-equipped locomotives accumulated slightly lower mileages than those with German-built engines, although, judging by the delivery dates, the difference was marginal. *John Beckett.* (Kodachrome, 8ASA)

Right: Lowest mileage of the 'D6xx' fleet was predictably achieved by the last delivered, No D604 *Cossack*, seen here passing Sprey Point, on the Teignmouth sea wall, with a largely carmine-and-cream rake making up the 6.25am Penzance–Paddington on 18 June 1959. Only six months old at this stage, the locomotive would accrue just 480,000 miles in traffic before the class was laid up just eight years later. *K. L. Cook / Rail Archive Stephenson* (Kodachrome, 8ASA)

Right: Newly ex works and in mint condition, No D819 *Goliath* passes West Drayton hauling its first train, the afternoon Paddington–Plymouth vans of 30 April 1960. The headcode appears slightly in error, because train 3C05 descibed the milk empties back to St Erth, while the 3C07 was the favorite running-in turn, the locomotive running under light load up to the capital and, if all was well, returning as far as Swindon with the vans train. Starting with No D813, the front end had been considerably tidied up by the replacement of the steam-age discs, lights and brackets with a neat four-character, two-piece headcode panel. *K. L. Cook / Rail Archive Stephenson* (Kodachrome, 8ASA)

*Above:*No D823 stands outside Swindon Works on 21 June 1960 in 'shop' green, which was significantly paler than the top coat which has yet to be applied. Fitters are hard at work all over the locomotive while an enthusiast films the proceedings. On the longest day of the year many of the workforce would be looking forward to the annual works holiday, which traditionally fell in the first two weeks of July. At the start of the great getaway in July 1960 17 special trains, bound for various seaside destinations, left Swindon between late on Friday night and 11.00 the following morning. One of the locomotives used was the completed No D823 *Hermes*, seen in action on 9 July with the 6.25am Swindon–Paignton and return. *Russell Leitch* (Perutz, 50ASA)

Right: "Could you tell me the number please, Mister?" An extremely rare picture of No D812, in 'shop' green and as yet un-named, working a service train. In pouring rain the locomotive awaits departure from Reading on 30 October 1959 with the 7.50am Taunton–Paddington via Bristol, on which the photographer was travelling. Why the locomotive had been pressed into traffic is unclear. No D812 was the last of an initial production batch of 10 after which significant alterations were made, most notably the inclusion of four-character headcode boxes neatly integrated into the nose. The locomotive was to have been named *Despatch*, the plates being cast but never fitted; instead it was named to commemorate the centenary of the Royal Naval Reserve.

Russell Leitch (Perutz, 50ASA)

Left: In July 1958 the North British Locomotive Co at Glasgow received an order for 33 B-B 'Warships' to the Swindon design but to be fitted with MAN engines and Voith transmission, the first of this series, No D833, being delivered in July 1960. While superficially identical in appearance to the Swindon built machines, there were a number of external detail differences, allowing identification of what would later be classified as Class 42s and 43s. This head-on view of No D835 *Pegasus*, approaching Laira Junction with train 3C16, the 9.00am Bristol-Plymouth vans train on 29 August 1961, clearly shows the 83A shedplate for Newton Abbot fitted to a raised backing plate on the buffer-beam. All North British-built locomotives carried the shedplate here, and, even when they fell out of use, the backing plates remained easily visible (see page 61), distinguishing NBL from Swindon-built machines; another distinguishing feature lay in the locomotive tail lights under the lamp irons, which were slightly inset when compared with the Swindon-built product. Those familiar with the area may wish to note that the little road bridge under which the train has just passed is now the site of the Marsh Mills flyover, while the fields to the left are occupied by a Sainsbury's superstore. *R. C. Riley* (Kodachrome II, 25ASA)

Right: Dick Riley made friends with many senior officers on the railway, who granted him permits for a variety of lineside locations as he pursued his hobby. This was the signalman's view from inside Laira Junction signalbox on 30 August 1961 as No D840 *Resistance* approached with train 1M95, the 7.30am Penzance–Manchester — a regular 'Warship' turn. A further four coaches, from Kingswear, would be attached at Newton Abbot. *R. C. Riley* (Kodachrome II, 25ASA)

Sonning Cutting has formed the backdrop for many pictures over the years, but, with the light value reduced significantly (even in high summer) by the deep cutting, colour pictures before the days of Kodachrome II are scarce. This is No D802 *Formidable* at the head of the down 'Royal Duchy' on 24 June 1961. Coach destination boards are still in place, but the headboard is absent; use of the latter was declining rapidly as the diesel age ushered in accelerated schedules throughout the day rather than on just a few prestigious trains. *John Beckett* (Kodachrome, 8ASA)

Being at the forefront of 'dieselisation' the Western Region was the first to encounter issues when operating the new motive power. One serious concern among trackside workers was the quiet approach of diesels, which often caught them unawares, and various experiments were conducted with the aim of increasing the visibility of approaching locomotives. No D845 *Sprightly*, outshopped from Swindon in August 1961, had a white band applied at roof level and its headcode doors painted yellow to create a warning panel, although this was soon found to be inadequate, and a much larger yellow panel became standard. The locomotive is seen at Bristol wearing its unique embellishments on 6 October 1962. Later No D857 also appeared with the small yellow panel, although this may simply have been the result of switching headcode-panel doors from a full-yellow-panelled sister during maintenance. *Tony Icke* (Agfa CT18, 50ASA)

London in the Swinging 'Sixties finds No D855 *Triumph* passing Westbourne Park with empty stock for Paddington from Old Oak Common, although the locomotive still displays the headcode for the up 'Mayflower'. RT buses on the bridge overhead and ventilated vans from Paddington's extensive goods yards complete the scene, recorded on 19 October 1963. *R. C. Riley* (Kodachrome II, 25ASA)

Left: Torbay may be renowned for its mild climate and sunny holidays in the English Riviera, but early in 1963 nowhere escaped the savage clutch of winter. On 11 February No D827 *Kelly* struggles through the snow at Torre with train 1N37, the northbound 'Devonian' — a favourite job for a Newton Abbot 'Warship' as far as Bristol, where diesel-electric traction would take over for the run to Bradford. *Peter Gray* (Kodachrome II, 25ASA)

Right: The early 'Sixties could perhaps be regarded as the heyday of Torbay as a resort, for the package holiday abroad was yet to make its mark. It was also the heyday of the 'Warships', for their bigger sisters had yet to oust them from the principal West Country services. On 18 June 1961 a Swindon 'Warship' at the head of the down 'Torbay Express' leads the 13-coach train beside the sea at Dawlish. Car enthusiasts will find plenty of interest parked in Marine Parade. *John Beckett* (Kodachrome, 8ASA)

Left: Those 'Warships' fitted with the original train-reporting discs were progressively fitted with four-character headcode boxes as they passed through works — but not before most had received the obligatory yellow panel. One of the last to be converted, No D810 *Cockade* pauses at Redruth on 15 September 1964 with the southbound 'Cornishman' from Sheffield (Midland) to Penzance. *David Pool* (Kodachrome II, 25ASA)

Above: Twelve coaches with a luggage van rather curiously marshalled in the middle make up the down 'Mayflower' (4.30pm Paddington–Plymouth), seen passing White Waltham at speed behind No D822 *Hercules* on 24 March 1962. The train was advertised as including through coaches for Kingswear and Truro, which probably accounts for the complex make-up. The locomotive, with the standard yellow panel, was the first of the Swindon batch to receive this, following repairs in January 1962. *Trevor Owen* (Kodachrome II, 25ASA)

In the autumn of 1964 control of the ex-SR route west of Salisbury became the responsibility of the Western Region, and 'Warships' took over the downgraded Waterloo–Exeter route. The service was sparse, but at least it had been spared the Beeching axe — although only just, much of the line now being singled. Nevertheless, 'Warships' were noted for putting in some lively performances over the route which they would now dominate for the next seven years. On Sunday 18 March 1966 No D826 *Jupiter* races west through Fleet with the 13.00 Waterloo–Exeter, comprising a mix of Mk 1 and Bulleid stock. *David Pool* (Kodachrome II, 25ASA)

Today's visitors to the Dartmoor Railway should recognise this scene, as the station at Okehampton, on the ex-LSWR route to Plymouth, has been carefully restored. Less fortunate was No D802 *Formidable*, seen pausing with the 10.40 Plymouth–Brighton on a glorious spring day, 28 May 1966. The locomotive has now lost its stencil brackets in favour of a four-digit headcode and carries no headboard clips.

The short handrails below the cab windows originally fitted to the three Pilot Scheme machines have been replaced with the longer standard version (see page 20).
The yellow warning panel is almost flat-topped compared with that on the majority of locomotives, both green and maroon, which had a discernible peak.
Tony Icke. (Agfa CT18, 50ASA)

27

Left: No D808 *Centaur* crosses Meldon Viaduct with the 10.40 Plymouth–Brighton on 2 July 1966. The train is running on the original trestle following strengthening, the up-line trestle having been closed earlier in the year. The viaduct was completed as a single trestle for the opening of the LSWR route between Plymouth and Exeter in 1874; four years later it was widened to allow double track by adding an almost identical structure alongside, and in later years the two viaducts were tied together to reduce sway. Nowadays a scheduled ancient monument, the cast- and wrought-iron structure underwent major refurbishment in 1996 and today forms part of the 'Granite Way' footpath / cycle track linking Okehampton and Lydford. *Dr I. C. Cantlon* (Kodachrome II, 25ASA)

Right: An altogether more substantial structure was the rebuilt Clinnick Viaduct, one of many to be found on the Cornish main line east of Bodmin Road, the new stone structure having replaced the timber original in 1879. Heading through the Glynn Valley, No D844 *Spartan* has a smart rake of Mk 1s in tow forming the 11.30 Penzance–Swansea High Street on 27 August 1966. *Peter Gray* (Kodachrome II, 25ASA)

Above: It had been standard practice in steam days to provide a pilot locomotive between Newton Abbot and Plymouth to assist over the notorious South Devon banks, and this continued for several years following the introduction of diesels. Dropping down Dainton Bank on 17 June 1967, No D6314 leads No D836 *Powerful* with 13 coaches forming train 1C28, the Saturdays-only 09.15 Bristol–Penzance. The MAN L12V18 engines fitted in both locomotives were not a success. Interestingly DB had not favoured MAN engines, only five locomotives being so fitted from new, the majority of its 'V200s' being powered by Maybach or Daimler-Benz. *Peter Gray* (Kodachrome II, 25ASA)

Right: Superpower for train 1M95, the 11.30 Plymouth–Manchester, in the shape of No D817 *Foxhound* and No D1012 *Western Firebrand*, waiting to leave Plymouth North Road on 3 April 1968. Both locomotives have recently received full yellow ends, a job that was undertaken only during visits to Swindon Works because trade-union agreements limited the amount of painting that could be carried out by depots. *Terry Nicholls* (Ektachrome X, 64ASA)

Above: Unique among the 'Warships' was No D830 *Majestic*, which was chosen to trial the then new Colchester-built Paxman Ventura 12YJXL engine in place of the Maybach MD650 powerplant. Not only was there no requirement for the Paxmans to be pre-heated; they were also slightly more powerful, being rated at 1,200hp each. Although this locomotive covered significantly fewer miles than did other members of the class, it must have impressed, because further engine orders followed for other BR types, and a later development of the Ventura — the Valenta — was chosen to power the world-beating High Speed Train. In this panned view *Majestic* is captured at speed passing Langstone Rock at Dawlish Warren with the 10.50 Cardiff–Paignton on 10 June 1967. *David Pool* (Kodachrome II, 25ASA)

Above right: No D831 *Monarch*, one of two early blue repaints with small warning panels, approaches Southampton with the 13.12 Poole–Swansea on 1 July 1967. The locomotive would almost certainly work only as far as Bristol before handing over to a 'Hymek' or Brush Type 4, because crews from South Wales generally were not trained on the 'Warships'. *Tony Icke* (Agfa CT18 50ASA)

Right: Despite a lack of traction knowledge amongst local crews the 'Warships' were still regular visitors to the South Wales main line as far as the Margam area with general goods and coal traffic. On New Year's Day 1969 No D868 *Zephyr* rumbles through a deserted Cardiff Central with coal empties. The locomotive has a maroon front skirt pinched from one of its sisters during repairs. *Russell Leitch* (Agfa CT18, 50ASA)

No D818 *Glory* basks in the sun at Bristol Bath Road on 3 August 1965. Fresh from overhaul at Swindon following derailment damage, this locomotive was one of the last 'Warships' to be outshopped in green before maroon was adopted for further repaints from September of that year. Buffer-beam and nameplate are now finished in pillar-box red, while the works plate has been painted in duck-egg blue to match the waistband; the warning panel is the most common shape, sloping upward to a point on those locomotives retaining the central lamp iron. Following withdrawal *Glory* became famous through being retained on the turntable at Swindon until 1985, when, just after the official announcement of the works' impending closure, it was suddenly cut up. *Terry Nicholls* (Kodachrome II, 25ASA)

34

The driver of No D817 *Foxhound* awaits the 'right away' at Bristol Temple Meads on 6 July 1971. Data panels were applied to all locomotives from the late summer of 1968, although the three Pilot Scheme locomotives did not survive long enough to receive them. The shed allocation sticker is displayed as a rectangular blue-backed sticker proclaiming NEWTON ABBOTT 83A. *Russell Leitch* (Perutz, 50ASA)

A close-up of the cabside of No D814 *Dragon* at Bristol Temple Meads on 16 September 1967. Serif lettering remains, and, while a neat stencil behind the cab door displays 84A, the shedplate down by the buffer declares 83A! The locomotive had been transferred to Laira from Newton Abbot in June of that year but in March 1970 would return to the main 'Warship' base at the latter shed. *Russell Leitch* (Agfa CT18, 50ASA)

Above: No D838 *Rapid* leaves the busy Tavistock Junction Yard with train 6M64, the 10.10 St Blazey–Warrington, on Wednesday 9 December 1970. *Bernard Mills* (Ektachrome X, 64ASA)

Right: No D841 *Roebuck* snakes slowly out of Hackney Yard displaying 0B29, the headcode for a light-engine movement to Exeter. On this occasion — 13 June 1967 — there is plenty of freight, including sheeted clay and mineral wagons bound probably for Exeter Riverside. The train is about to pass under the bracket controlling the approach to Hackney Yard and Newton Abbot, which still has wooden signal arms. No D841 was one of the last North British B-B 'Warships' to receive a green repaint, emerging from Swindon in July 1965. *Peter Gray* (Kodachrome II, 25ASA)

37

Shortly after return from overhaul at Swindon, No D600 *Active* stands at Laira on 14 June 1967. *Active* was the second and final A1A-A1A 'Warship' to be outshopped in corporate blue and the only one to be finished with full yellow ends, although the numbers were still in the non-standard serif face. By this date the original 'Warships' were confined almost exclusively to Cornwall and had regular diagrams involving freight traffic from Tavistock Junction Yard to Truro and Ponsandane. Considering the level of freight today, it is hard to believe that Plymouth had two extensive yards, at Friary and Tavistock. In the mid-'Sixties the latter alone generated sufficient traffic to warrant three mandatory return trips every 24 hours to Cornwall, so with parcels traffic and conditional clay working there was more than enough to keep the 'D6xxs' occupied. Their very different cab layout meant that, by this date, only a handful of Penzance and Laira men were trained on them, confining their use to the Duchy. *David Percival* (Kodachrome II, 25ASA)

Left: In the summer of 1967, with South Wales short of traction, it was decided to use Nos D601/2/4 on traffic from Margam. This seems a strange decision because, in terms of maintenance and traction knowledge, staff in South Wales were familiar only with the Maybach-engined 'Hymeks' and 'Westerns'. The North British machines were different in just about every respect, so it is no surprise that during their short (10-week) stay they worked very few trains. This is the only known colour picture of No D602 *Bulldog* on the Central Wales line and shows the locomotive after arrival at Llandrindod Wells in September 1967 with train 6J81, a pick-up freight from Landeilo Junction Yard, which it worked on only two occasions. Sadly the negative has long since been lost, this image being re-scanned from the original print.
Roy Palmer (Kodacolor)

Right: Almost certainly the last colour photograph taken of a working A1A-A1A 'Warship'; No D602 *Bulldog* is less than 48 hours away from being switched off for good as it passes St Budeaux West on 28 December 1967 at the head of train 1A77, the 12 noon Penzance–Paddington. Contrary to popular belief, the three members that returned from South Wales in November went straight back into front-line service in Cornwall, and all were working before being driven onto the scrapline at Laira on the morning of Saturday 30 December. *Terry Nicholls* (Ektachrome X, 64ASA)

39

Above: Winters have become much warmer in recent years, but snow was once a regular feature even in the West Country. Arriving at Exeter with a good overnight covering on 9 December 1967 is No D807 *Caradoc* with the 09.00 from Waterloo. *Geoff Lendon* (Agfa CT18, 50ASA)

Right: Nos D827 *Kelly* and D829 *Magpie* wait for time at Exeter St Davids with the 08.30 Plymouth– Paddington on 18 March 1968. This was before the introduction of the accelerated timetable in May of that year, but in the preceding months locomotives were often trialled as a pair on this service, to check the reinstatement of the multiple-working connections and the feasibility of the new timings. *Russell Leitch* (Agfa CT18, 50ASA)

Left: Ilfracombe was a regular destination for 'Warships', and on summer Saturdays in the 'Sixties there were still through workings to Paddington. Here No D820 *Grenville* departs from the terminus on a hazy Saturday in August 1968 and passes the now closed engine shed. Facing a gradient of 1 in 36 from a standing start for the first 2½ miles, this was the steepest climb out of any British terminus. It was compounded by some sharp curves past Lower Slade before the summit of the line was reached near Mortehoe. Most steam services were double-headed and limited to five coaches. With Load 9 behind the locomotive, *Grenville*'s driver will already have the controller wide open. The line was to close on 5 October 1970. *Bernard Mills* (Ektachrome X 64ASA)

Above: Tavistock once boasted two stations, but today the bustling market town is completely isolated from the railway network. This is Tavistock North, on the old LSWR route from Plymouth to Lydford via Bere Alston. Steam oozes from leaking connections as No D809 *Champion* awaits departure with the Plymouth–Brighton service in February 1967. Very soon this everyday scene would be consigned to history, the last Plymouth–Brighton through working via Okehampton running just days later, on Saturday 4 March 1967. Traction for the last up service was sister No D810 *Cockade*, and participants were treated to a sparkling run, a speed of 89mph being achieved near North Tawton. In retrospect the closure of this fast main-line route, which avoided the exposed coastal section of the GWR route via South Devon, was desperately short-sighted. *Bernard Mills* (Ektachrome X, 64ASA)

The battered state of No D864 *Zambesi* on 10 January 1971 is typical of the condition in which most 'Warships' could be found. The locomotive has just been turned at Old Oak Common and is about to take the exit road, leaving behind No D838 *Rapid* in an equally tatty condition. The horn grilles may be clearly seen under the buffers, and — unusually for a Class 43 — the multiple-working equipment appears to have been left in place, although whether by this time it was still functioning is another matter. *Tom Rogers* (Kodachrome X, 64ASA)

For a short period in the autumn of 1967 some North British 'Warships' were transferred to the Midlands to release Brush Type 4s from the Birmingham–Paddington corridor. Despite extensive crew training the experiment was short-lived owing to poor reliability, and the Class 47s were back on the route by the end of the year. On 22 October 1967 No D848 *Sultan*, one of the very early casualties of the fleet, enters Leamington Spa with a service for Paddington. Withdrawal came in March 1969 with just 537,000 miles on the clock, the lowest of any Class 43. *Bryan Hicks* (Agfa CT18, 50ASA)

The short reign of the 'Warships' on the Birmingham route coincided with major remodelling of Paddington station, some services being diverted into Marylebone. Here, on 11 November 1967, No D846 *Steadfast* has arrived in the unfamiliar surroundings of the latter terminus at the head of train 1V08. Bags deposited by the crew stand on the platform, along with the inevitable white enamel billy-can for tea! *Bryan Hicks* (Agfa CT18, 50ASA)

Above: A major revamp and acceleration of the West of England timetable introduced in May 1968 saw the 'Warships' tasked in pairs for selected services. A stud of 18 Swindon Class 42s had their multi-unit equipment checked over and reinstated as necessary for a series of complex cyclic diagrams. On the humid afternoon of 30 July 1968 the noise from four Maybachs would have been something to savour as Nos D831 *Monarch* and D808 *Centaur* restarted train 1A59, the 14.30 Plymouth–Paddington, away from the station stop at Westbury.
The Rev Alan Newman (Kodachrome II, 25ASA)

Right: The versatility of the 'Warships' is evident in this view of No D822 *Hercules* pulling away from Clink Road Junction signalbox on 20 September 1970 with 25 tipplers from the nearby Merehead Quarry. Early concerns that the light weight (just over 78 tons) of the 'Warships' would provide insufficient brake force on partially fitted freight trains were mitigated as more of the remaining freight traffic became fully fitted. As traffic from the Mendip Quarries grew, the 'Warships' and their larger sisters, the 'Westerns', were preferred over contemporary diesel-electrics because of their high tractive effort upon starting and at low speed.
The Rev Alan Newman (Kodachrome II, 25ASA)

Even with two locomotives and four engines things didn't always go according to plan. After a fine morning the rain has set in at Cullompton on Tuesday 3 September 1968 as the down 'Cornish Riviera' (10.30 Paddington–Penzance) with train locomotives Nos D867 *Zenith* and D819 *Goliath* is assisted past construction work for the M5 motorway by No D7067. The 'Hymek' is believed to have come on at Taunton, as both 'Warships' were in trouble, and upon arrival at Exeter all three locomotives were replaced for the onward journey by No D1072 *Western Glory*. *Peter Gray* (Kodachrome II, 25ASA)

In trouble, part 2! On 29 May 1967 No D804 *Avenger*, on the up 'Cornish Riviera' at Par, has decided to give up, and assistance, in the shape of No D808 *Centaur*, which has come off St Blazey shed, is backing onto the front under the watchful eye of the guard. Of particular note is the first coach, a Hawksworth vehicle repainted in corporate blue and grey — one of only a handful of ex-GWR passenger vehicles to wear this livery. *Peter Gray* (Kodachrome II, 25ASA)

While the Eastern and London Midland Regions tended to favour-double heading their Royal Train workings as insurance, the Western was quite happy to turn out a single locomotive — usually a 'Warship' or a 'Western'. On 15 July 1966 an immaculate No D806 *Cambrian* passes Eastleigh conveying HM The Queen and HRH The Duke of Edinburgh, who had traveled overnight from Truro after a day of engagements in Cornwall. Complete with sleeping cars and a generator vehicle, the heavy train is heading for Bournemouth Central. Such workings would carry a traveling fitter and utilise a locomotive recently 'shopped' at Swindon Works; *Cambrian* had emerged from overhaul at the end of June and so was just nicely run in. *Les Elsey* (Agfa CT18 50ASA)

Above: Seen from Western Tower at Plymouth on 9 June 1970, No 813 *Diadem* passes with the ECS from a short Royal Train which overnight, headed by No 810 *Cockade*, had conveyed HRH The Prince of Wales from Paddington to St Austell for a tour of Duchy estates. *Bernard Mills* (Ektachrome X, 64ASA)

Right: No D821 Greyhound leaves the decaying terminus at Devonport Kings Road on 8 March 1968 with the Royal Train carrying HRH The Duke of Edinburgh to Plymouth North Road for a visit to open the School of Maritime Studies. Having travelled overnight from London behind No D1023 *Western Fusilier*, the train had been berthed at Kings Road in the early hours and was the last to use this short branch before closure. *Bernard Mills* (Ektachrome X, 64ASA)

Only two 'Warships', Nos D808 and D810, lasted long enough in green to receive full yellow ends. This is the latter, *Cockade*, pausing at Exeter with a vans train on 3 June 1969. Underneath the dirt the paintwork appears in reasonable condition, although in those days paint technology, combined with the effects of salt spray and abrasive wash plants, was such that a new coat lasted little more than 2-3 years before significant deterioration set in. *Russell Leitch* (Agfa CT18, 50ASA)

Another unique machine was No D870 *Zulu,* instantly recognisable because of its roof-mounted horn cowling. All the main-line hydraulics were fitted with the same Desilux two-tone horn, making their approach easily distinguishable from the Region's diesel electrics. The last Swindon-built machine, No D870 was subjected to a series of experiments, particularly with a view to fitting the class with electric train heating, although space constraints would preclude this. On 21 June 1969 No D870 approaches Britannia Crossing on the Dart Estuary with the 10.42 Paignton –Kingswear local, the stock returning as the 09.55 Kingswear–Paddington.

Gerry Batchelor (Agfa CT18, 50ASA)

No D870 *Zulu*, this time in harness with No D869 *Zest*, catches the attention of locals in Marine Parade, Dawlish, as it leaves with the 14.30 Paddington–Penzance on 12 July 1969. The pair had worked up earlier in the day on the 06.10 from Penzance and would end their cycle on the up newspapers as far as Plymouth. *Terry Nicholls* (Ektachrome X, 64ASA)

Left: Creeping out of the undergrowth at St Budeaux East, No D6303 has been brought to a stand at the exit signal with a train from Bull Point MoD depot in June 1967. One of the original six Pilot Scheme North British Type 2s, the locomotive shared aspects of its design and a number of mechanical components with the larger A1A-A1A 'Warships'. Following North American practice, it had been intended that, in addition to working local passenger and freight traffic, disesel locomotives could be used in multiple, two or three being coupled together for more demanding traffic. By the time the first 'D63xx' locomotives were delivered in 1959, at a cost of £55,000 each, the thinking had changed somewhat, although they did work in multiple — particularly in Cornwall — during the early years. Mechanically they were essentially half a 'D6xx', some rather unsatisfactory styling giving the appearance of a chopped-off nose end. The production locomotives that followed were substantially different, with uprated engines and a more compact transmission, and the little family of prototypes were left to potter around the far West, where their idiosyncrasies were understood. *Terry Nicholls* (Kodachrome II, 25ASA)

Right: At Bristol Bath Road in April 1968 No D6313 receives attention from the depot's re-railing gang as well as from various onlookers, who have presumably turned up to offer moral support! Hydraulic jacks are being used to recover the locomotive, which has somehow managed to end up straddling the pointwork. From this angle the similarity to the original North British 'Warships' is readily apparent, but in contrast with their bigger sisters the design was hardly elegant. *Terry Nicholls* (Kodachrome II, 25ASA).

M.O.D. PROPERTY KEEP OFF

A light dusting of snow covers the landscape as No D849 *Superb* approaches Adlestrop with the 13.15 Paddington–Hereford on 7 March 1970. Disappearing in the distance is No 833 *Panther* with the 14.15 Worcester–Paddington. The North British Class 43s were the regular traction for this line, the Swindon-built Class 42s making only very occasional appearances. Given a train frequency of less than one every two hours, it was quite remarkable to secure a crossing shot such as this. *Bryan Hicks* (Kodachrome X 64ASA)

On a warm summer's evening in June 1970 No D851 *Temeraire* approaches Charlbury with the 16.15 Worcester–Paddington. Modellers may wish to note that roof patterns on the 'Warships' varied, the most noticeable difference being the fan housing over the cooler groups. With the exception of Nos D833/4/61 the remaining Class 43s had the fan cover enclosed in a raised steel rim (as seen in this view), with walkways abutting the circumference; most Swindon-built machines — the exceptions being Nos 832/67-9 — had a flush fan cover, with a longitudinal walkway across the whole cover. The exits from the exhaust stacks on the Class 43s were slightly offset because of the configuration of the MAN engines. Further differences in the roof detail on the NBL and Swindon locomotives involved the covers atop the various types of train-heating boiler. *Gerry Batchelor* (Agfa CT18, 50ASA)

Left: No D6334 passes Newton Abbot with an additional westbound vans train just after 17.30 on Monday 27 April 1970. *Bernard Mills* (Ektachrome X, 64ASA)

Above: No 6339, one of the regular Exeter-outbased Class 22s, ambles along the Culm Valley line near Coldharbour with milk tanks from Hemyock bound for Tiverton and Exeter on 8 March 1969. The line had closed to passengers in September 1963 but remained open for grain and milk traffic plus the occasional oil train bringing fuel for the dairy. Initial diesel traction was a 204hp shunter, but by 1968 the line had been strengthened to allow 'D63xxs' and the odd 'Hymek'. The curtain for the North British Type 2s came down on New Year's Day 1972, this locomotive working milk tanks from Hemyock, while sister No 6333 was employed to collect milk from Chard; both locomotives were switched off after arrival back at Exeter. *Bernard Mills* (Ektachrome X, 64ASA)

Above: In the Limpley Stoke Valley on the approach to Freshford — a location well known to photographers today — No D844 *Spartan* ambles north on 4 July 1969 with a Wimbledon–Severn Tunnel Junction freight conveying a bit of everything, as was typical of the period. Empty coal wagons from the concentration depot at Wimbledon are towards the rear of the train, which had picked further traffic at Salisbury and Westbury. *The Rev Alan Newman* (Kodachrome II, 25ASA)

Right: On 2 April 1970 No D836 *Powerful* found itself on a relatively unusual duty — the 15.23 Portsmouth–Cardiff, seen leaving Bradford-on-Avon. 'Warships' were regular visitors to the Eastleigh area, but Portsmouth was more likely to see the smaller 'Hymeks'. Long after shedplates had been abandoned, the raised fixing plate fitted only to the Class 43s is clearly visible to the right of the left-hand buffer. The rectangular blanking-plate by the right-hand buffer covers the original multiple-unit connection, which on most Class 43s was isolated to reduce fault-finding for maintenance staff. *The Rev Alan Newman* (Kodachrome II, 25ASA)

Left: No D845 *Sprightly* enters Lostwithiel station with the 07.55 Penzance–Paddington on 15 June 1967. Today's visitor will find the original cast GW station sign still in place, along with semaphore signals. *David Pool* (Kodachrome II, 25ASA)

Above: No D838 *Rapid* speeds through Dawlish Warren on 4 June 1969 with the 00.50 Manchester–Penzance conveying sleeping cars as the second and third vehicles. A small observer on the platform, the son of the photographer, waves to Grandfather, who is driving. Today the observer is an experienced driver working on the routes of the old Western Region. *Rapid* was one of the last 'Warships' to be repainted in maroon, in the autumn of 1966, before blue was adopted. Interestingly a visit to the works in August 1968 for the application of full yellow ends saw the locomotive receive another top coat of maroon, long after blue had become the standard. The locomotive survived until October 1971, when it was withdrawn still in this livery. Cutting-up, at Swindon, followed in July 1972. *Terry Nicholls* (Kodachrome II, 25ASA)

Left: Easing gently across Brunel's Royal Albert Bridge spanning the Tamar, Nos 814 *Dragon* and D822 *Hercules* enter Devon with the up 'Cornish Riviera' on 24 June 1969. By the 1969 timetable the rather expensive use of twin 'Warships' on selected services had been much reduced, after finding that in most cases a single 'Western' could keep time on the schedules. *Gerry Batchelor* (Agfa CT18, 50ASA)

Right: The seldom-seen corporate image of a matching pair of 'Warships' in the final BR blue livery with logo under the nameplate. No 814 *Dragon* leads No 829 *Magpie* through the reverse curves on the approach to Totnes on Tuesday 30 September 1969 with train 1A48, the up 'Cornish Riviera'. Four days later the summer timetable would finish, bringing to an end the booked use of pairs of 'Warships' on prestige services. *David Pool* (Kodachrome II, 25ASA)

Above: No D6333 leads No 810 *Cockade* through Dawlish Warren with train 6B59, the 14.50 Ponsandane– Exeter Riverside, on 14 July 1971. Booked to arrive at Riverside at 20.06, the train was scheduled to stop at Plymouth from 18.17 to 18.25 for a locomotive to be attached and was thus usually double-headed. The leading wagon carries compressor plant from Compair Maxam at Redruth, while further down the train is a white tank wagon carrying bromine extracted from seawater at the Associated Octel plant on the Hayle branch. *David Cobbe collection* (Ektachrome X, 64ASA)

Right: The headcode displayed by No 831 *Monarch* appears to be incorrect as the locomotive rounds the curve at Aller at 19.45 with train 7B44, the 18.35 Keyham–Exeter Riverside, on 29 July 1971; the displayed headcode of 7C10

described the 19.55 Exeter Riverside–East Usk. In the distance No D1064 *Western Regent* is coming off the branch with ECS from Paignton. Out of sight behind the photographer, No 869 was held at signals with a down freight 6B36 for Friary, awaiting a passage to follow another 'Thousand' just leaving Newton Abbot westbound with train 1B58. Ten minutes earlier 'Peak' No 185 had preceded No 831 with train 6A29, the 18.30 Plymouth Friary–Paddington sundries (including NCL traffic), while just in front of the 'Peak' Nos 6356 and 853 were teamed up on train 6B59, the 14.50 from Ponsandane. Four freights, one passenger, one ECS, all in the space of 20 minutes — and the up Paddington perishables (6A17) with No D835, the Acton milks with another 'Thousand' and the St Blazey–Stoke clay (6M55), with a returning No 869 piloting No D1019, were yet to come! *Peter Gray* (Kodachrome II, 25ASA)

No D844 *Spartan* arrives at Kingwear, having crossed Waterhead Viaduct (a rather grand title for such a modest bridge) with the 07.56 Newton Abbot–Kingswear, on 21 June 1969. This service provided the stock to form train 1E48, the 08.52 Kingswear–Leeds. At this date British Rail still owned two diesel ferries that plied across the water to Dartmouth station — one of the very few 'railway' stations in the country that never saw a train. Across the estuary stand the imposing buildings of the Britannia Royal Naval Training College. *Gerry Batchelor* (Agfa CT18, 50ASA)

Two years later and near the end of its short life, No 844 *Spartan*, now in blue, curves into Totnes on 13 September 1971 with train 6C26, the 08.45FX Plymouth Friary–Severn Tunnel Junction. Delivered in March 1961, the locomotive lasted just 10 years before withdrawal on 3 October 1971. The North British machines were always disliked by crews and maintenance staff, largely because of their troublesome MAN engines, which, although simpler than the Maybach design, were under-developed for rail application. Unlike the Maybachs they did not require pre-heating, but starting from cold often produced excessive fumes, which would blow back into the cab. *David Pool* (Kodachrome II, 25ASA)

Above: Recently outshopped from Swindon after its final overhaul, No 818 *Glory* approaches Basingstoke with train 1V15, the 13.00 Waterloo–Exeter. Walkways over the cooler-group fan covers are clearly visible, as are, at cantrail height above the nameplate, the additional louvered slots cut in one side only of Nos D813-65 'Warships' to improve air flow to the burners of the boiler. *Glory* was experimentally fitted from new with a horizontal-barrel Spanner Mk IIIa boiler which it would retain until withdrawal. *Bernard Mills* (Ektachrome X, 64ASA)

Right: As late as 25 September 1971 Salisbury still boasted many relics from the steam age. No D817 *Foxhound*, which survived in maroon until withdrawal just a week later, approaches from the west with the 10.10 Exeter–Waterloo. *David Pool* (Kodachrome II, 25ASA)

PASSENGERS MUST
NOT CROSS THE LINE

PLEASE
USE SUBWAY

Left: No 832 *Onslaught* pauses at Churston on 7 August 1971 with the 16.05 Kingswear–Newton Abbot, having worked down earlier with the 11.30 from Paddington. No 832 is shown in the records as the last 'Warship' to be withdrawn, but this can be misleading, because the locomotive was put aside in early November 1972 as a candidate for eventual use by the Railway Technical Centre at Derby and never worked again for BR. The oft-quoted withdrawal date of 16 December 1972 thus represented little more than an administrative transaction, and it was *Onslaught*'s move to Derby that would prolong its life, leading to eventual preservation. *Peter Gray* (Kodachrome II, 25ASA)

Above: The shadows are lengthening on 5 August 1971 as No 812 *Royal Naval Reserve 1859-1959* approaches Aller Junction at 19.25 with train 4B10, the 15.53 Bristol Temple Meads–Plymouth vans — a regular 'Warship' working at the time. *Peter Gray* (Kodachrome II, 25ASA)

73

Above: Ready to leave Long Rock depot with train 6B59, the 15.05 Ponsandane–Exeter Riverside, No 841 *Roebuck* begins its last week in traffic on Sunday 26 September 1971. The locomotive is showing the tell-tale signs of oil leaks for which the MAN engines in the Class 43s were well known. *Roebuck* was on its second coat of blue, having originally been outshopped with emblems at each cab end. Storage came in late 1969, when No 841 was laid up at Old Oak Common for several months before reinstatement and a trip to Swindon in the spring of 1970; the legacy of its allocation to the London depot is visible below the headcode panels. Two small circular grilles have been cut to try to improve ventilation through the cab and clear it of fumes. Most of the Class 43s based at Old Oak were treated to this modification, although there was a wide variety of shapes and positioning. The locomotive was finally condemned as part of the mass withdrawal which took place on 3 October 1971. Spared joining the long lines of withdrawn hydraulics

congregating at St Philips Marsh, No 841 worked light-engine as train 0F76 from Laira to Newton Abbot, where it collected condemned stablemates Nos 6326 and D6343 before towing them to Swindon Works as train 0F73. *Terry Nicholls* (Ektachrome X, 64ASA)

Right: No 811 *Daring* pulls out of the loop at Dawlish Warren with the 13.00 Avonmouth–Plymouth Friary on 16 June 1971. Of the three crew members occupying the cab all appear to have cups of tea to hand, the second man's brew being visible atop the control cubicle. While the 'Warships' had a number of flat surfaces on which to deposit cups, spills from hot sugary tea did little to improve the operation of the Brown-Boveri control gear housed within. With some faults the electricians soon learned exactly where to look! *Terry Nicholls* (Ektachrome X, 64ASA)

Railway enthusiasts have a fascination with last-ever runs, and on 3 October 1971 the 'Warships' bowed out from the Waterloo–Exeter line, handing over to the SR-based Class 33s.

The final up service was behind No 823 *Hermes*, seen here pausing at Salisbury with train 1O18, the 18.20 Exeter St Davids– Waterloo. A trail from the shunter's lamp has been left during the long exposure. Upon arrival at the London terminus the locomotive worked light to Old Oak Common, where it was switched off for good. *Bernard Mills* (Ektachrome X, 64ASA)

That just left the down working, the 1V19 19.08 Waterloo–Exeter, to make the Salisbury call behind No D822 *Hercules*, seen with a line of 'Cromptons' ready for the following morning's workings. On arrival at St Davids the locomotive ran round and took the ECS as train 5B80 to Newton Abbot, where it was formally withdrawn. 'Warships' would never again work the Waterloo–Exeter services. *Bernard Mills* (Ektachrome X, 64ASA)

A bird's-eye view, recorded on 30 October 1971, of Bristol St Philips Marsh, which at the time was a DMU-servicing facility. Almost every siding is occupied by withdrawn hydraulics following the mass slaughter that had taken place on 3 October. Beginning in the top left-hand corner and working from left to right are Nos 845/34/58, surrounded by Class 22s, whiles the three 'Warships' near the centre of the picture, with BR personnel in front, are Nos 867 *Zenith* (still with nameplate),

854 and 826 (with hand tail-lamp attached); behind No 867 can be seen the roof of maroon No 815, attached to three Class 22s (the last of which is No D6318), followed by Nos 868 and D819. In all the sidings were host to 17 'Warships' and 15 Class 22s on this date. Centre stage, Pressed Steel suburban unit No 408 is about to pull forward from the rather primitive facility. *Terry Nicholls* (Ektachrome X, 64ASA)

Only 13 'Warships' would survive to see active service in 1972, all from the production batch of Swindon-built locomotives. Passenger work was much reduced, and the survivors were now found largely on a variety of parcels and freight work. Although small and lightweight, they were strong locomotives, which fact enabled them to be regularly employed on the heavy stone workings from Merehead Quarry.

On 6 July 1972 No *821 Greyhound* climbs through a cutting near Gomshall, on the North Downs line, with train 6014, the 08.55 Westbury–Gatwick service bringing aggregates for construction of the M23 and M25 motorways. *Trevor Maxted* (Kodachrome II, 25ASA)

Sydney Gardens in Bath is the location for another view. No 821 *Greyhound* this time with a mixed and lengthy load making up train 7B68, the 15.30 from Westbury to Bristol West depot on 22 June 1972. The 'D8xxs' had been the WR's brainchild for the Modernisation Plan and were significantly ahead of their time. They introduced the industry to advanced techniques of stressed-skin body construction, and during their short lives they consistently ran up to 40% greater mileage than their diesel-electric contemporaries, and at much higher load factors; only the 'Deltics' could boast more miles per annum — but at a price. Chief Engineer at Swindon Sam Smeddle and his team had contributed greatly to British diesel development, but in so many ways the locomotives were doomed to an early grave.
The Rev Alan Newman (Kodachrome II, 25ASA)

The premature demise of the 'Warships' meant that the class very nearly escaped preservation. Attempts to save No D601 while it languished at Barry ultimately came to nothing, while No 821 was saved largely by default; first choice for Colin Massingham and Chris Reid had been one of the sad-looking North British Type 2s, No 6319, purchase of which had been secured through the Stores Controller at Derby, but communication failure within BR saw the locomotive cut up by mistake at Swindon, whereupon Colin was offered the much larger 'Warship' as a gesture of appeasement. No 821 *Greyhound* thus became the first main-line diesel to be privately preserved, moving first to Didcot and then to Reading Gas Works, where restoration commenced ahead of a move to Swindon. From 1981 it made its home on the North Yorkshire Moors Railway, the by-now-restored locomotive being seen here at Levisham on 6 June 1983 in charge of the 15.50 Grosmont–Pickering breakdown train, which included Drewry 0-6-0 diesel shunter No D2207. At the time of writing No D821, owned by the Diesel Traction Group, is based at Bridgnorth, on the Severn Valley Railway. *Hugh Dady* (Kodachrome 64)